THE WORLD IS FULL OF A** HOLES

By K.L. Harris

Illustrated by Nik Henderson

Make-Believe Press

K.L. Harris is a writer, author, and all-around make-believer.
Harris normally writes novels about adventures in fantasy worlds, but this is a book she needed to write, at a time when it felt like the world needed it too.
To find out more about K.L. Harris you can visit her website at, **www.masterofmakebelieve.com**

Nik Henderson grew up in Missouri, and studied illustration at the Savannah College of Art & Design in Georgia. He currently works in both the animation and book illustration industries, with past clients including Dreamworks Television Animation and Red Star 3D. In his spare time, he loves to paint outdoors, write, and hike.

Library of Congress Control Number: 2020920910

ISBN: 978-1-7323686-9-9

First Edition, November 2020

MAKE-BELIEVE
—— PRESS ——

www.make-believepress.com

Dedicated to anyone who has ever encountered an Asshole.
-K.L. Harris

To the guardians in my life.
-Nik Henderson

The world is full of Assholes.
I'm sure you've encountered one or two,
And if you haven't, you will, no matter what you do.

It's inevitable that someone, somewhere,
Will be rude and disrespectful to you.
Sometimes, it will even be those you're closest to.

(Double rude.)

And sometimes it won't.
Sometimes it will be someone in passing,
Or someone you've only met that day.

Sometimes it will be obvious, and other times,
You won't recognize an Asshole straight away.

They're found in unexpected places
Or hidden behind phony social graces.
Lurking 'round every bend,
Waiting for their moment to offend.

So be ready for when they do,
Because they'll do their best
To do the worst by you.

And sometimes, they'll be successful too.

There will be times
When an Asshole will make you ashamed of your differences.
They'll convince you you're less than you are.
They'll cut you down for getting too big, too good,
Or for reaching too far.

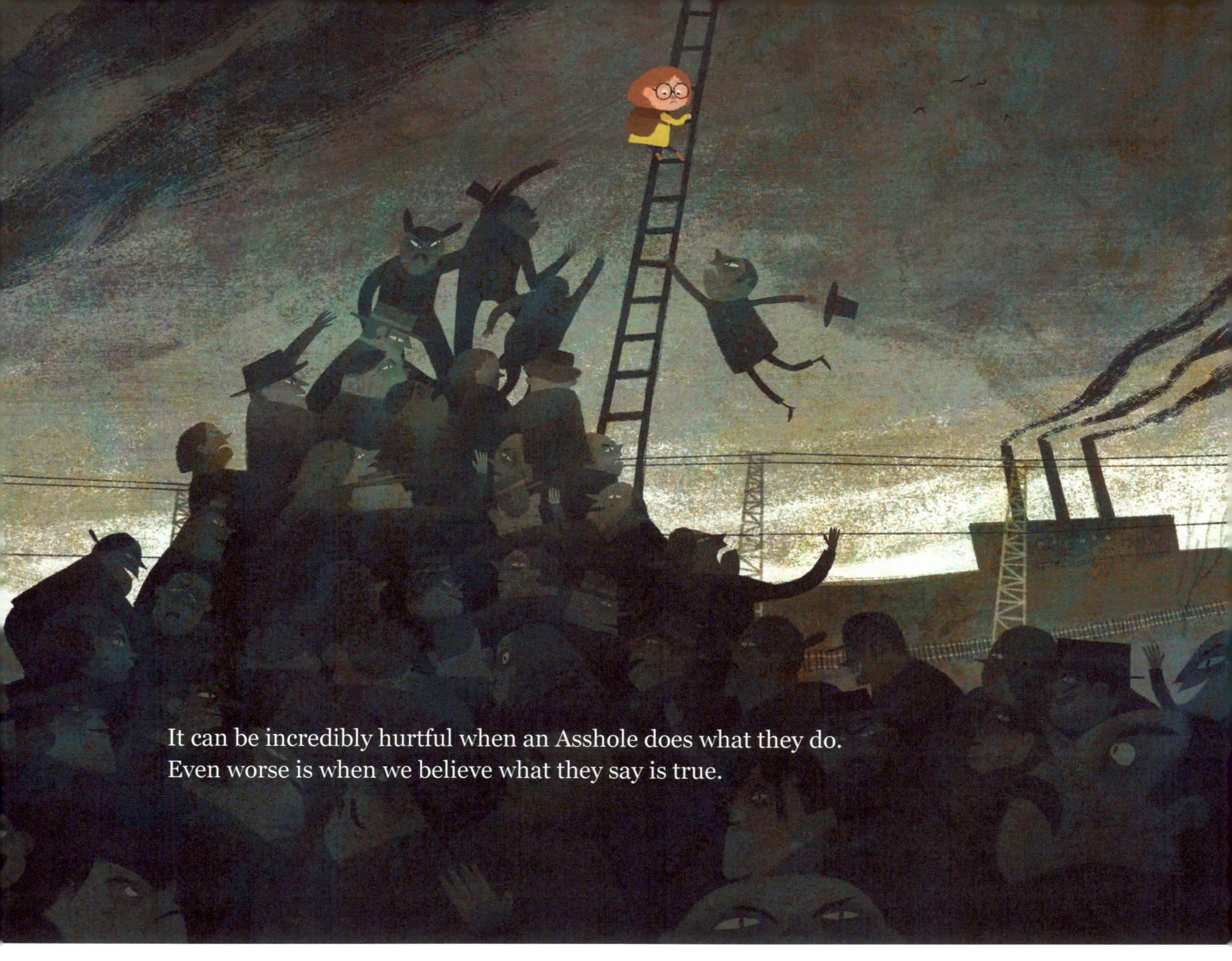

It can be incredibly hurtful when an Asshole does what they do.
Even worse is when we believe what they say is true.

But **it's not**.

So don't let them get to you.
Just remember, the problem is *them*, **not you.**

The trick is to spot them and name them for what they are,

ASSHOLES!

If you remember that, their damage can't go far.

How can you identify an Asshole? you might ask.
That's tricky, because you'll find them behind every mask.

MAJOR

They come in every age, from the old to the new.
You can't pick them by color, they aren't partial to hue.

Assholes don't favor a gender either
They offend, whether they're a him or a her,
Or undecided or in between.
Makes no difference to the Asshole gene.

Assholes can be doctors, teachers, or people scooping ice cream.
Professions can't keep someone from being malicious or mean.

We can't pin them to a social class.
No amount of wealth, education, or elocution
Can prevent someone from being an ass.

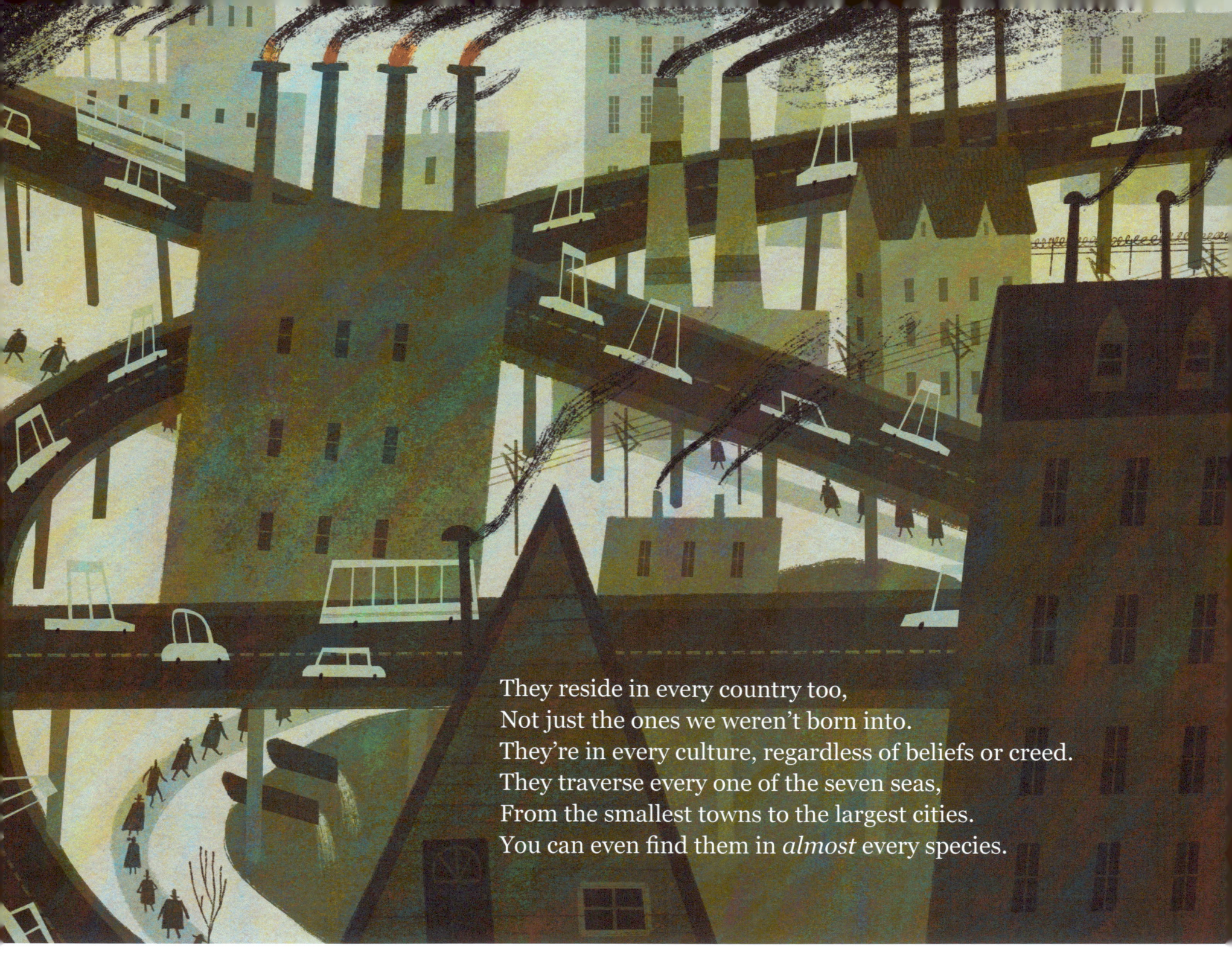

They reside in every country too,
Not just the ones we weren't born into.
They're in every culture, regardless of beliefs or creed.
They traverse every one of the seven seas,
From the smallest towns to the largest cities.
You can even find them in *almost* every species.

The only way to truly classify an Asshole is by what they do.
You'll know them by the way they treat others
And by how they treat you.
To give an example, here's listed a few.

CHARACTERISTICS OF AN ASSHOLE:

- Tromps on feelings
- Singles out
- Lies
- Cheats
- Does dirty dealings
- Exploits kindness
- Always puts themselves first
- Doesn't care if they make someone else's life worse
- Tells people one thing, and when their back is turned, says another
- Makes jokes at someone else's expense
- Insults fathers or mothers...

The list goes on, but I think you get the idea.
Remembering these traits will help make who you're dealing with clear.

Now that you can identify an Asshole and know what to look for,
Be sure to show them straight to the door.
You can say, "Stop, that's enough.
You're an Asshole. I don't need this rotten stuff."

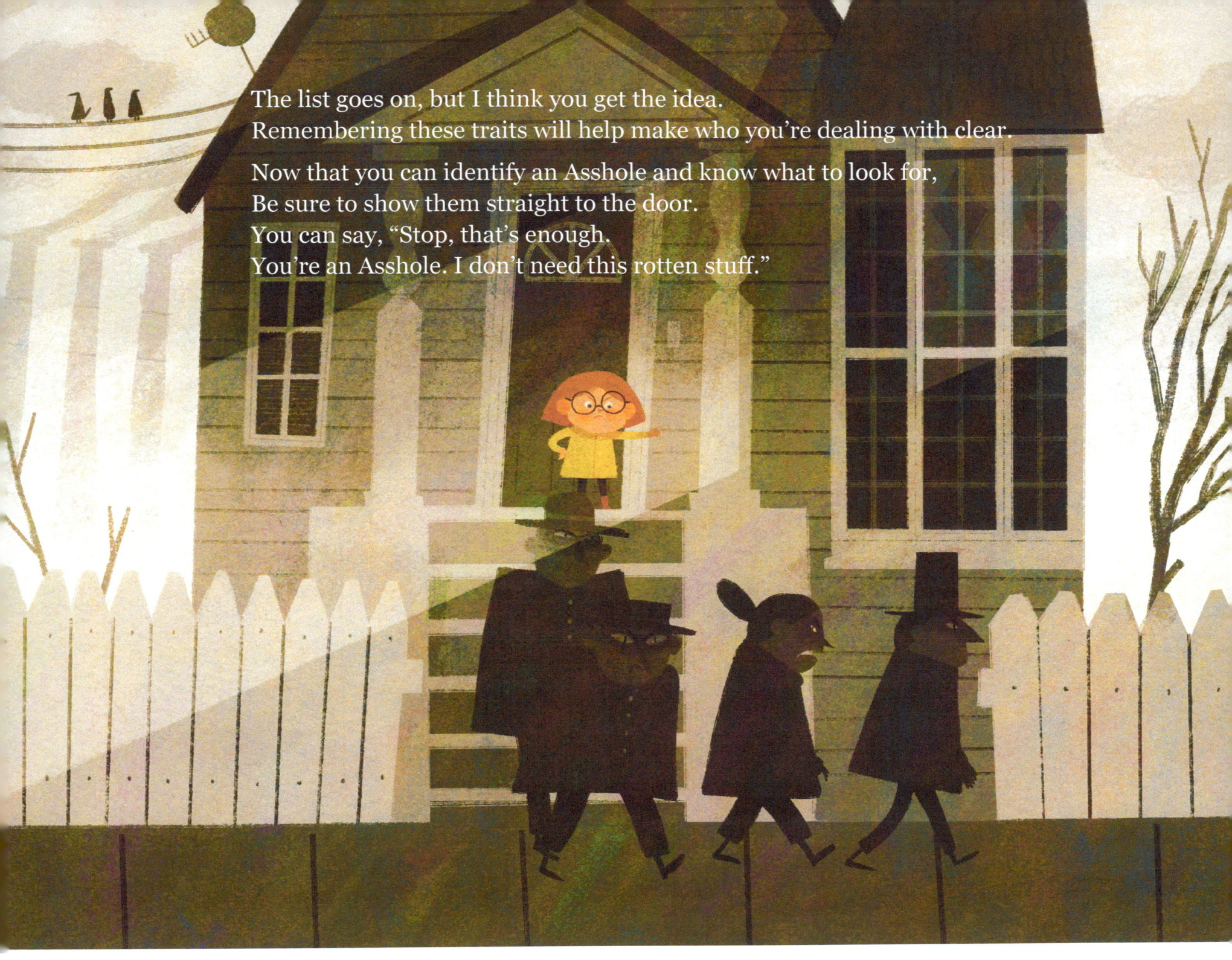

Yes, it's true, the world is full of Assholes,
And they're here to stay.
Festering like that dish at the back of your fridge tray.
As irritating as the residue left from that sticker you pulled away.
As imposing as that houseguest who should've left yesterday.
As offensive as smelly old gym socks that haven't been washed since last May.

But don't let this worry you. You're going to be fine.
Quite frankly, Assholes aren't worth your time.

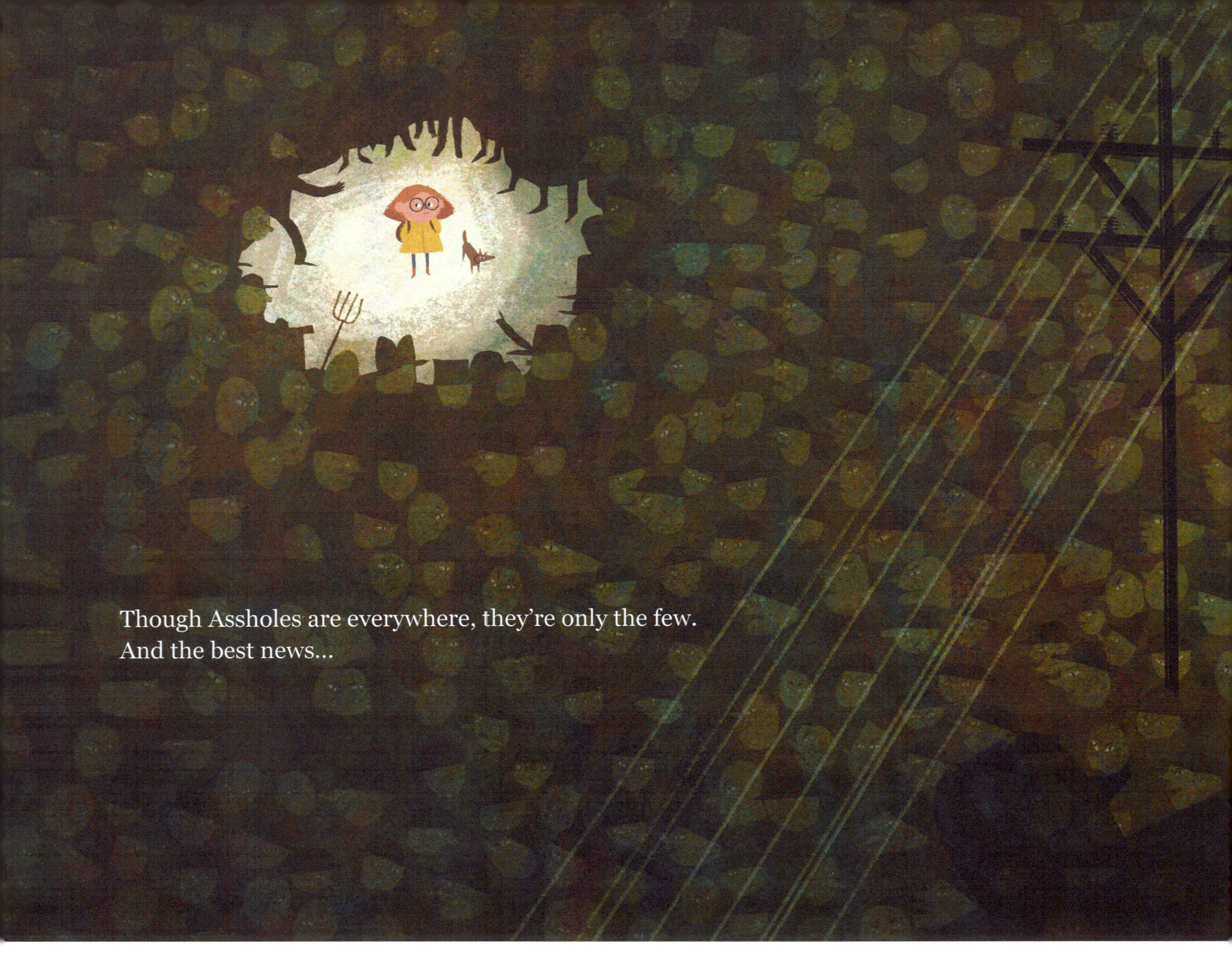

Though Assholes are everywhere, they're only the few.
And the best news...

The world is full of something else that *is* worth paying attention to.

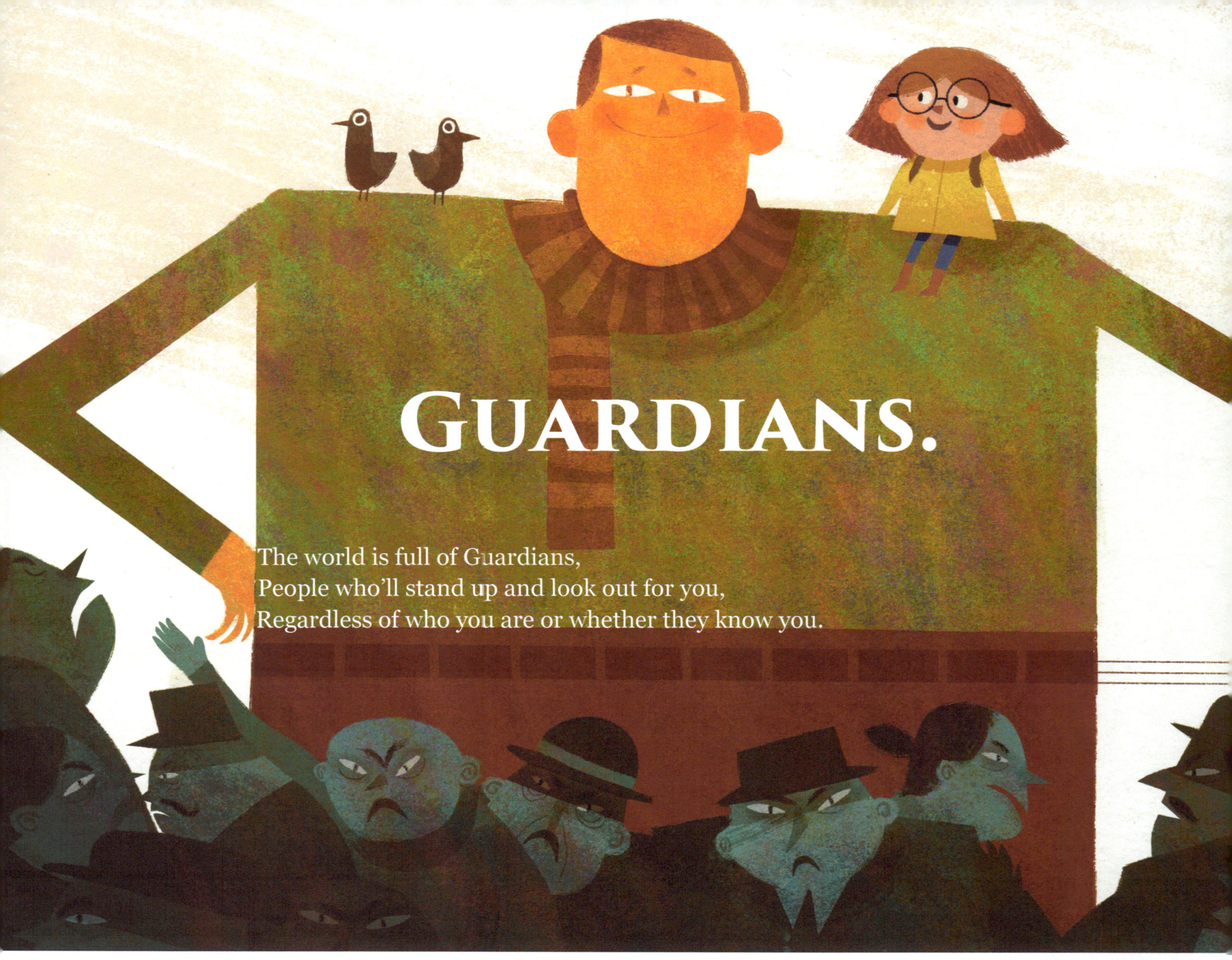

GUARDIANS.

The world is full of Guardians,
People who'll stand up and look out for you,
Regardless of who you are or whether they know you.

People who'll speak up when you're not treated right,
Catch you when you're falling, defend you in a fight.

Give you a hand up when you're down,
Give you directions when you're from out of town.
Give you a roof over your head,
Somewhere to sleep when you're in need of a bed.

People who'll always have a nice thing to say,
Who'll cheer you up when you're having a bad day.

Someone who helps take your pain away.

Someone who loves you for you,
Regardless of how you look or what you do.
People who won't judge you for being who you are,
Who'll cheer you on and encourage you to go far.

Guardians fill our world. You'll find them wherever you go,
Whether you're at home or foreign places you don't know.

How do you spot a Guardian? you might ask.
That's tricky, because they can be found behind every mask.

Guardians come in every age, from the old to the new.
They come in every color too.

And don't think that they favor a gender.
People can defend, whether they're a him or a her
Or undecided or in between.
Makes no difference to the Guardian gene.

Some people flaunt being a Guardian, and others don't need to be seen.
They work as doctors, teachers, even people scooping ice cream.

You'll find them in every culture, regardless of beliefs or creed
They traverse every one of the seven seas,
From the smallest towns to the biggest cities.
You'll even find them in *almost* every species.

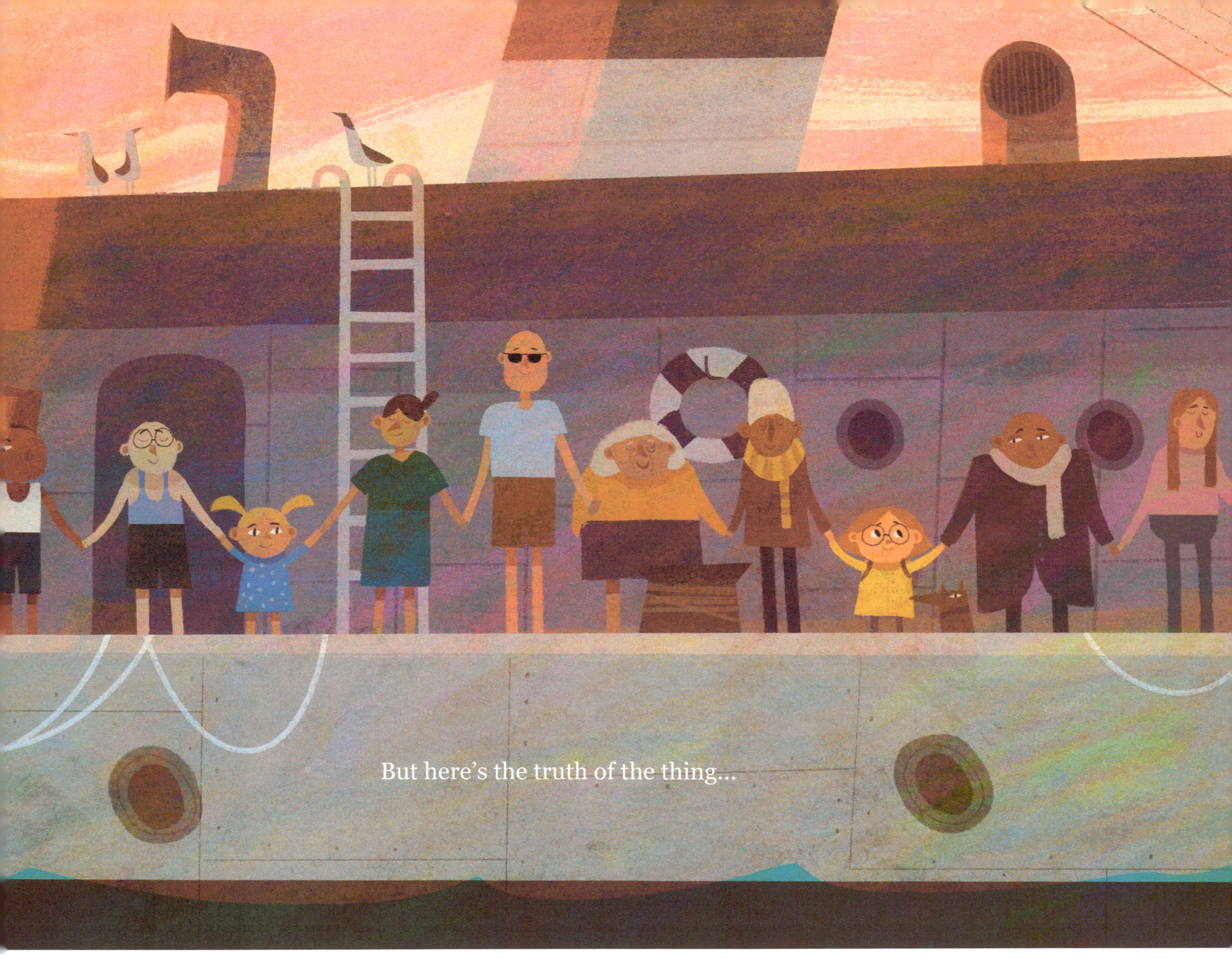

But here's the truth of the thing...

There's both Asshole and Guardian in you and in me,
Both Asshole and Guardian in all human beings.

What defines us and sets us as one or the other
Is who we choose to be and how we treat each other.

So, which will you be?
What path will you take?
Every moment of every day, it's your choice to make.

www.ingramcontent.com/pod-product-compliance
Lightning Source LLC
Chambersburg PA
CBHW040712150426

42811CB00062B/1879